DO NOT REMOVE
CARDS FROM POCKET

Michael Faraday

Any one of Michael Faraday's discoveries in physics and chemistry would have placed him in the front rank of scientists. In fact, his work ranged over such a wide field that it forms the basis of the whole of modern science.

Through remarkable good fortune, this village blacksmith's son managed to become laboratory assistant to Sir Humphrey Davy. Faraday made such an impression on him that the following year, 1813, he took him on a Grand Tour of Europe on which he met many of the leading scientists of the day. In 1827, he became Davy's successor at the Royal Institution. As a physicist, he built the first "magneto-electric" motor, pioneering the study of electricity and magnetism. The supply of electricity to our homes and all kinds of electric motor, from hairdryers to vacuum cleaners, electric drills to milk floats, owe their existence to Michael Faraday.

Brian Bowers tells the story of this generous, charitable and devoutly religious scientist, carefully explaining technical matter. The book contains more than fifty diagrams and illustrations as well as a date chart, glossary, reading list and index.

BRIAN BOWERS, B.Sc.(Eng.), A.K.C., C.Eng., M.I.E.E., was born in 1938 and educated at the Royal Grammar School, High Wycombe and King's College London. He is a chartered electrical engineer and a member of the Royal Institution. After five years as a Examiner in the Patent Office he joined the staff of the Science Museum where he is now a Deputy Keeper in the Department of Electrical Engineering and is also responsible for the Museum's publications. He has written two Museum booklets and various historical articles relating to electrical engineering.

Pioneers of Science and Discovery

Michael Faraday
and Electricity

Brian Bowers

Deputy Keeper in the Science Museum

Other Books in this Series

ISBN 85078 132 9

Copyright © 1974 by Brian Bowers
Second impression 1978
Third impression 1980
First published in 1974 by
Wayland Publishers Ltd., 49 Lansdowne Place, Hove,
East Sussex BN3 1HF

Printed and bound in Great Britain at The Pitman Press, Bath

Contents

List of Illustrations

1 *Early Life*

Michael Faraday has been called "the Father of Electricity," and the highest award given by the Institution of Electrical Engineers is the Faraday Medal. Faraday was a village blacksmith's son, who became the greatest scientist of his time, a Fellow of the Royal Society and recipient of many awards and honours.

The Surrey village of Newington, where Michael Faraday was born on 22nd September 1791, is now part of Greater London. Michael was the third child of James and Margaret Faraday. They had recently moved south from Westmorland. He had an elder sister Elizabeth, born in 1787, and a brother Robert born in 1788. The family soon moved again, north of the River Thames, and lived at various addresses in what is now West London. Another sister, Margaret, was born in 1802. James Faraday was in poor health and unable to work full-time. He died in 1810, and Mrs. Faraday took in lodgers until her sons could support her. Michael Faraday's early years were hard, and he had little formal education. In later life he said: "My education was of the most ordinary description, consisting of little more than the rudiments of reading, writing, and arithmetic at a common day school. My hours out of school were passed at home and in the streets."

In 1804 Michael went to work as an errand boy for Mr. George Riebau, a bookseller and bookbinder. One of his duties was to deliver newspapers, and in some cases to collect them back. In those days, many people could not afford to buy a newspaper, and so paid to read one which had to be returned. The following year, when he was fourteen, Michael was apprenticed as a bookbinder and bookseller to Riebau.

The house in Jacob's Well Mews where Faraday lived as a boy.

George Riebau's bookshop, where Faraday was apprenticed as a bookbinder.

Nothing is known about his life in the first few years of his apprenticeship, but he became a competent bookbinder and many volumes bound by him are still in existence. This practical training in working with his hands stood him in good stead in later years, when great skill with laboratory apparatus was vital to his scientific work. He read many of the books which he bound and became interested in science, especially chemistry and electricity. In his spare time he made chemical experiments, and built a frictional electric machine which is still preserved at the Royal Institution in London.

Walking in the City of London one day, he saw an advertisement for a series of evening lectures on "natural philosophy" (the nineteenth-century term for pure science). The lectures were given by a Mr. Tatum who led a group called The City Philosophical Society. The meetings were held in his house

on Wednesday evenings. Tatum gave a scientific lecture with demonstrations every two weeks, and on the other, alternate Wednesdays one of the other members would speak. Faraday joined the Society early in 1810, with a shilling fee paid by his brother Robert who was by then a working blacksmith.

The City Philosophical Society was really a secondary school for Faraday. During the years 1810 and 1811, he heard lectures on all kinds of subjects—chemistry, electricity, hydrostatics, optics, mechanics, geology, astronomy. Here also he met Benjamin Abbott, a young Quaker who worked in the City. The two became close friends. Much of our knowledge of this part of Faraday's life comes from his letters to Abott which still survive.

Faraday took detailed notes of Tatum's lectures and later wrote out the lectures in full, sometimes noting that he disagreed with Tatum about something. On at least one occasion he made his disagreement known in the discussion after the lecture, and was then invited to address the Society. The point in dispute was the nature of electricity. Most scientists thought that electricity was an "imponderable fluid" (a fluid having no weight) which could pass through solid objects. (Heat and magnetism were explained in a similar way.) The question was: were there two electric fluids, one positive and one negative? Or was there a single fluid?

Tatum thought that electric effects were caused by a single fluid which was always present in some quantity. Too much produced a positive electric charge, and too little a negative one. Faraday's lecture, which was written out in full, sets out the arguments for there being two electric fluids. This was the first talk in public given by the man who was to become the greatest scientific lecturer of his time.

One of Mr. Riebau's customers, a Mr. Dance, was impressed with Faraday's interest in science. He gave him tickets to hear Sir Humphry Davy lecturing at

Faraday's frictional electric machine which he built in his spare time while working as a bookbinder.

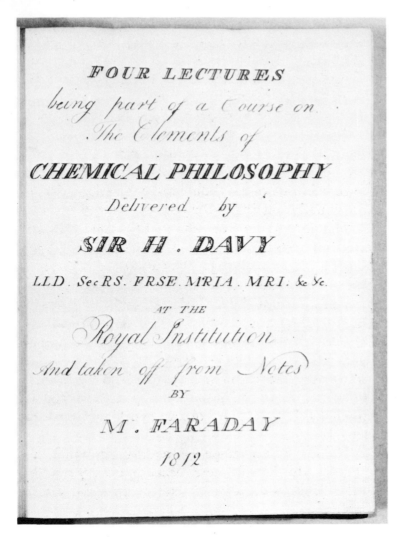

FOUR LECTURES
being part of a Course on
The Elements of
CHEMICAL PHILOSOPHY
Delivered by
SIR H . DAVY
LLD. Sec RS. FRSE. MRIA. MRI. &c &c.
AT THE
Royal Institution
And taken off from Notes
BY
M . FARADAY
1812

Title page of Faraday's notes on
Sir Humphry Davy's lectures at
the Royal Institution.

the Royal Institution. Following his practice at the
City Philosophical Society, Faraday took detailed
notes, which he bound himself. Later he was to send
the bound volume to Davy with a letter asking for a
job in any scientific capacity.

Throughout his life Faraday kept a series of "common place books" or notebooks in which he jotted
down facts, quotations, ideas and questions as they
came to him. One note, written in 1822, explains the
value of such books: "I already owe much to these
notes, and think such a collection worth the making

by every scientific man. I am sure none would think the trouble lost after a year's experience."

The earliest one, kept in the Library of the Institution of Electrical Engineers in London, is described on its first page as: "A collection of Notices, Occurrences, Events, etc., relating to the Arts and Sciences, collected from the Public Papers, Reviews, Magazines, and other miscellaneous works. Intended to promote both Amusement and Instruction and also to corroborate or invalidate those theories which are continually starting in the world of science."

The notes tell us something of the range of Faraday's interests and his sense of humour. He quotes the *Liverpool Courier* of 1823: "*Walking the streets.*—It has been found a difficult thing at Liverpool to make the townsfolk adopt the well-known and useful rule of keeping the right-hand side of the path in walking; and reason having failed, an attempt has been made to shame them into obedience to it, the following courteous placard having appeared on the walls of the town: '*Respectable people* are requested to keep the right-hand side of the footpath and Blackguards the left.'"

There is also a recipe for making gin which it is pointless to reprint here because Faraday added afterwards: "I suspect . . . that there is some mistake in the quantities!"

2 *The Royal Institution*

Benjamin Thompson (1753–1814) was an American scientist and politician. He travelled widely and was given the title Count Rumford by the King of Bavaria.

While living in London, Rumford led a group who founded the Royal Institution of Great Britain (usually known simply as the Royal Institution) in 1799. It was created "for diffusing the knowledge and facilitating the general introduction of useful mechanical inventions and improvements, and for teaching by courses of philosophical lectures and experiments the

The Royal Institution of Great Britain, 21 Albemarle Street, London, in 1881.

application of science to the common purposes of life." It has been described as a sort of technical school, but that is not an adequate description.

The founders hoped that wealthy patrons would finance the Institution, and that the working classes would attend to learn how to apply science "to the common purposes of life" in their work. It was also the intention to give lectures which interested the upper classes, and since the Institution depended entirely on their money the lectures for them became the more important.

Sir Humphry Davy (1778–1829), a Cornish surgeon and chemist, became lecturer in chemistry and geology at the Royal Institution in 1801 and was appointed Professor in the following year. He was a brilliant speaker. His courses on such subjects as agricultural chemistry, or the art of tanning, drew the fashionable society of London. They may sound mundane subjects to us, but the Managers of the Royal Institution chose them because they wanted to encourage the use of science in farming and business. Davy's eloquence helped to save the Institution from bankruptcy, and the reputation he gained from his chemical discoveries helped that of the Institution.

During his first years there, Davy worked on chemistry and electricity. He obtained the metals potassium, sodium, calcium, strontium, barium and magnesium for the first time by using electricity to decompose their oxides. In 1808 he received the Napoleon prize of 3,000 francs for his electrical researches, despite the fact that Britain and France were at war. In 1812 he was knighted by the Prince Regent, and he was made a baronet in 1818. He is best known for his invention in 1815 of the miner's safety lamp. Davy also tried without success to break down chlorine, and concluded it must be an element. This was the man whom Faraday heard lecturing on chemistry four times in 1812.

On 7th October 1812, Faraday's apprenticeship

Overpage "Scientific Researches! New Discoveries in PNEUMATICKS! —or—an Experimental Lecture on the Powers of Air!"
A cartoon by James Gillray of a pneumatic experiment at the Royal Institution at the end of the 18th century.
Humphry Davy (1778–1829) is shown holding the bellows, while Benjamin Thompson, Count Rumford (1753–1814), stands smiling on the right.

with George Riebau came to an end. He began work as a journeyman bookbinder for a Mr. De La Roche. De La Roche seems to have been a difficult master, which made Faraday consider seriously whether he might find a career in science. He wrote to Sir Joseph Banks, the President of the Royal Society, asking for a scientific job, but received no reply. However, later in October 1812 Davy was temporarily blinded by an explosion in the laboratory. Faraday was introduced to Davy—possibly by Mr. Dance—and worked for Davy for a few days as a secretary.

After this Faraday wrote to Davy asking for a scientific post, and sending the volume he had made of Davy's lectures. There was no vacancy at the time, but when a laboratory assistant, William Payne, was dismissed for brawling, Davy sent for Faraday and offered him the job. The Managers of the Royal Institution formally decided, on 1st March 1813, that "Michael Faraday be engaged to fill the situation lately occupied by Mr. Payne on the same terms." The terms were a salary of one guinea a week with two rooms at the top of the Institution, fuel and candles supplied.

An artist's impression of Humphry Davy trying out his miner's safety lamp.

3 European Tour

Although he was only a laboratory assistant, Faraday's abilities were quickly recognized. His first work was preparing various substances in the laboratory, but he was soon helping with demonstrations at the various lectures given in the Institution.

Faraday had never been abroad and in fact he had never travelled more than twelve miles from London. In 1813 Sir Humphry Davy resigned his Professorship (though he was then made Honorary Professor of Chemistry) to make a tour of Europe, and offered to take Faraday with him. The sons of the English aristocracy usually finished their education by going on the "Grand Tour" of Europe with their tutors. The son of a blacksmith could never have hoped for such an educational experience, but Michael Faraday had the chance to go, with Davy as his tutor. The tour lasted eighteen months, and while they were away Faraday learned French and Italian. He met many of the leading scientists of France, Switzerland and Italy, discussed their work with them and formed lasting friendships.

The idea of making the tour at that time must have seemed foolish to many people, for Britain and France were at war. Yet Napoleon willingly allowed the English party to travel through France, and Sir Humphry and Lady Davy and Faraday left London on Wednesday 13th October 1813. There were personal difficulties on the way, since Lady Davy insisted on treating Faraday as a servant although Sir Humphry was looking on him more and more as a scientific colleague.

They travelled first to Plymouth. Faraday kept a *Journal* in which he recorded his wonderment at the scenery, especially in Devon, which was so unlike any-

Michael Faraday as a young man.

thing he had seen around London. On the Friday, two days after setting out, he referred to "the mountainous nature of the country" in Devon, and added: "this day gave me some ideas of the pleasures of travelling and have raised my expectations of future enjoyment to a very high point."

They sailed to the French port of Morlaix, which gave Faraday a poor impression of France. After passing through the Customs (which he thought very slow and inefficient) they acquired horses and set off for Paris. In Paris, Michael Faraday saw all the tourist sights, and went with Davy on his visits to chemists, laboratories and factories. His *Journal* makes several comparisons between England and France, such as "French apartments are highly ornamented, English apartments are clean." After shopping in Paris he wrote, "It would seem that every tradesman here is a rogue."

Early in November they visited a sugar factory where sugar was extracted from beet. Faraday's first task at the Royal Institution had been to extract sugar from beet in the laboratory, so he was eager to see the process on an industrial scale. This was not just a scientific curiosity. Making sugar from beet was of great economic and political value because it gave Britain a home-grown source of sugar. Most of Britain's sugar came from sugar-cane grown in the West Indies. This made sugar an expensive commodity, and the supply routes were easily attacked by an enemy in the time of war.

The climax of their stay in Paris came later in November when three of the most distinguished French scientists, Ampère, Clément and Desormes, called on Davy to show him a new substance obtained from a certain seaweed. It had been discovered a couple of years previously by Bernard Courtois, who made washing soda from the ashes of burned seaweed. When the new substance was heated it gave off a purple vapour; this condensed to give shiny dark

A sugar factory in France such as Faraday visited on his European tour with Humphry Davy in 1813.

crystals of the substance. The French chemists soon found that it behaved rather like chlorine. Chemists, however, disagreed about the nature of chlorine. Most believed it was the oxide of an unknown substance, while Sir Humphry Davy, as we have seen, thought it was an element. Davy set to work with the portable chemical set which he always took on his travels.

Faraday was about to witness an important piece of chemical research. It was more than the discovery of a new element: one of the basic beliefs held by most chemists was being challenged. Most chemists believed that all acids contained oxygen. Indeed, the name "oxygen" means "acid maker." Since chlorine formed an acid (hydrochloric acid) when combined with hydrogen, they believed it must be an oxide. Davy did not accept the oxygen theory of acids, and he believed that chlorine was an element. After several experiments, including an attempt to decompose the new substance by electricity, Davy concluded that what the French chemists had given him was also an element. Still in Paris, he wrote a paper to the Royal Society in London describing the new substance and proposing the name *Iodine* for it.

After Christmas, 1813, the party left Paris and continued the journey southwards. During a stay at Montpellier, Faraday casually walked into a fort on a hill above the town. Afterwards he wrote in his *Journal*: "The stroll round the ramparts was pleasant, but I imagine that at times whilst enjoying myself I was transgressing for the sentinels regarded me sharply." Faraday had no interest in politics, and it probably never occurred to him as strange that he, an Englishman, should be free to wander around a French fort just when it was about to face an attack by an army under the Duke of Wellington!

The party travelled on through Italy, reaching Florence in April. Here, Faraday was interested to see the telescope with which Galileo had discovered the satellites of Jupiter. Sir Humphry Davy turned to another scientific problem: the nature of diamond. The Grand Duke of Tuscany had a large burning glass which could be used to burn diamonds by concentrating the rays of the sun. The point of using a burning glass was that it allowed Davy to make the experiment inside a large closed glass vessel, so that he could collect the products of combustion without risking contamination. He confirmed that the only product was pure carbon dioxide, and concluded that diamond was not *chemically* different from graphite and lamp-black (which also gave carbon dioxide when heated), but was just a different crystalline form of the same element.

They toured Rome and visited Naples, where they climbed Mount Vesuvius and Davy explained the geology of volcanoes to Faraday. The Queen of

Sir Humphry Davy (1778–1829) was Professor of Chemistry at the Royal Institution when Michael Faraday became an Assistant in the laboratory. Davy resigned in 1813 to make a European tour on which he took **young** Faraday.

The giant battery built by
Humphry Davy in the basement
of the Royal Institution.

Naples gave Davy some specimens of colours from the
ruined Roman city of Pompeii, which Davy analysed.
This was probably the first use of chemistry in archae-
ology, and it also marked the end of the tour. Davy
decided to return home and the party reached
London in April, 1815.

While they were in Naples, Davy had also given
some advice about the task of unrolling and restoring
a number of Roman papyrus manuscripts found at
Pompeii. It was suggested that Faraday might stay
there to do some more research on the papyri, possibly for several years, but the idea came to nothing.

4 *Faraday the Chemist*

On returning to England, Michael Faraday was employed again by the Royal Institution. He was now Superintendent of the Apparatus and Assistant in the Laboratory and the Mineralogical Collection. He had a salary of thirty shillings per week and rooms in the Institution building. He was now a much more important member of the staff than before his travels. His duties included setting up lecture demonstrations for the Institution staff, especially W. T. Brande, who had succeeded Davy as Professor of Chemistry. Faraday also helped Brande with his commercial analytical work, and soon became a skilled analytical chemist himself. Faraday's first scientific publications were on analyses—the very first being the *Analysis of Native Caustic Lime of Tuscany* (1816).

In the few years after his return Faraday embarked on a massive task of teaching himself chemistry. Among his books which survive to this day are three volumes of Brande's *Manual of Chemistry* (1819), which Faraday broke apart and rebound with blank pages interleaved with the text. He spent many hours in the Library studying scientific journals and filling the blank pages with detailed notes and references.

Faraday gave a series of lectures to the City Philosophical Society, beginning in January 1816. During this period of his life he made a close and critical study of all the lectures he heard, to master the art of lecturing himself. His *Advice to a Lecturer*, a collection of his notes and letters on the art of lecturing published in 1960, is an excellent handbook for teachers and lecturers today.

In 1823 Faraday obtained liquid chlorine for the first time, using a method suggested by Davy. He heated chlorine hydrate in one arm of a closed tube shaped like an upside-down V. The chlorine gas driven off condensed to liquid in the other arm of the tube, which was kept cold. He then liquefied a number of other gases in the same way.

As his reputation grew, Michael Faraday was in demand as a scientific consultant and expert witness in legal cases. In 1818 a Mr. S. Cocks engaged Faraday to help him in a lawsuit about a patent. In 1820 he gave evidence for some insurance companies in a complicated case which arose from a fire in a sugar refinery: was the fire started in the sugar itself, or in a certain oil which was used in the refining process? According to the sugar company, neither the oil nor the vapour from it could catch fire at a temperature below 580° Fahrenheit. Faraday made tests for the insurance companies and found that the vapour could catch fire at the much lower temperature of 382° Fahrenheit.

The case was decided on other grounds, but the experience had two important results for Faraday. Davy had given evidence for the sugar company, and the incident helped to drive the two men apart. While

Faraday in his laboratory at the Royal Institution in the 1860s.

doing his research for the insurance companies, Faraday had become interested in the gases given off when oils are heated. At about the same time, his elder brother Robert had begun to work in the new gas industry in London. The Portable Gas Company sold gas made by heating whale oil, or codfish oil, in a furnace. The gas was stored in high-pressure containers (about thirty times atmospheric pressure). The containers were carried round to the customer's house and used for supplying gas lighting. The Gas Company found that during the bottling process a liquid collected in the apparatus. In 1825 Michael Faraday was asked to analyse this liquid. He found that it was a mixture of substances which evaporated at different temperature, but most of it was a liquid which boiled at about 186° Fahrenheit. This, he concluded, must be a single compound. He found by analysis that it was a compound of carbon and hydrogen only, and he found the ratio of the two elements in it. He called the new substance "bicarburet of hydrogen" (known today as benzene).

Benzene is a substance of basic importance to organic chemistry. It is the simplest substance to have a "ring" structure. That is, some of the atoms in the molecule are arranged in a ring rather than in a line:

C   carbon atom
H   hydrogen atom

The importance of benzene was only realized in 1860 when Kekulé worked out its structure. Faraday deserves the credit for finding a new substance, but he could not have known its significance.

As the son of a blacksmith, Faraday was naturally interested when in 1818 a London cutler, James

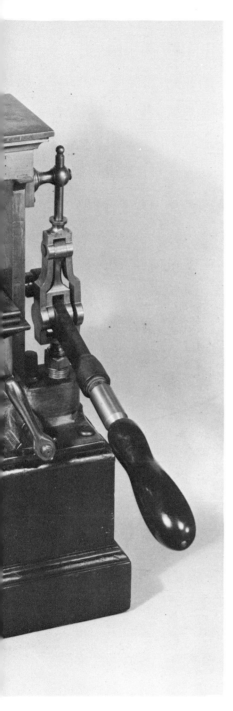

Faraday used this press to force water out of crystals of benzene.

Stodart, sought help in some researches into steel. Stodart's shop sold "Surgeon's Instruments, Razors and other Cutlery" made from wootz. This was a steel imported from India. Stodart found it better for his purposes than any steel made in Europe. For more than twenty years he had been trying to make a steel as good or better than wootz, but without success. As a member of the Royal Institution he must have known Faraday, who willingly analysed a specimen of wootz and then tried to manufacture some. But the work failed, and was abandoned for some months.

However, about this time Faraday was engaged by a South Wales ironmaker to analyse samples and then invited to visit the works. Faraday was always pleased to visit factories and workshops. In July 1819 he set out on a walking tour of Wales, beginning with Mr. Guest's iron works where he spent several days, and also including Mr. Vivian's copper works near Swansea. The diary of his journey includes a description of the South Wales countryside as well as a detailed account of the production of iron and copper.

When Faraday came back to work with Stodart on steel, he had a new idea: copper was hardened by alloying it with one of the "noble" metals, gold or silver. Could steel be hardened in the same way? He built a more powerful furnace, and then melted iron together with a little platinum, rhodium, silver, nickel and tin. He examined the alloys formed. He found that they could indeed produce in the laboratory steels which were better than any steel commercially available in England. The next step was to persuade a steel manufacturer to use this process on a large scale. A firm in Sheffield did try to use the new alloys to make high-quality cutlery, but it was not a success, probably because the alloying metals were so expensive.

James Stodart died in 1823, and Faraday lost interest in steel. But the work with steels showed that Faraday was well qualified for another research task.

29

In 1824 the Royal Society decided to sponsor some research into optical glass, to build an improved telescope. The work was entrusted to John F. W. Herschel the astronomer, George Dollond the optician, and Michael Faraday. Faraday had the practical task of making various kinds of glass. First he studied the processes involved, and analysed various glass samples. Then, in September 1827, a special

Sergeant Anderson of the Royal Artillery, who was employed in 1827 to assist Faraday, in the laboratory at the Royal Institution.

laboratory equipped with a furnace was provided for the research at the Royal Institution. An assistant, Sergeant Anderson of the Royal Artillery, was engaged to help Faraday with the work.

Glass is made by heating together a number of substances including sand, potash or soda, and usually lime, magnesia or lead oxide. Faraday was trying to make a very heavy glass, with as much lead as possible. It was thought that this would have the best optical properties. The work was beset with difficulties. Often, when the samples were examined after cooling, he found the glass was cracked, or contained bubbles or bands of colour where the ingredients had not mixed properly. If he stirred the molten glass in the furnace the pot containing it usually broke. He tried using a platinum dish to hold the mixture in the furnace, but whenever a drop of molten glass splashed onto the iron supports the lead oxide in the glass reacted with the iron, leaving pure lead metal. Unfortunately, lead reacts with platinum to form an alloy which melted in the furnace. So whenever any of the lead touched the dish it reacted —and left a hole in the dish. Several times Faraday put in his notebook that the "bottom of the platina vessel disappeared . . . and the experiment was suddenly put an end to."

This was but one of many difficulties which Faraday had to face, explain and overcome. Finally, in April 1829, he produced a piece of glass which he could describe in his notebook as "good", and which George Dollond could make into a lens.

Faraday continued to work on glass sporadically for another couple of years, but by 1831 circumstances had changed. The finances of the Royal Institution had improved, and the income from the steel and glass research projects was no longer so important.

And Faraday himself wanted to devote his whole time to another topic: electricity.

5 *Faraday the Man*

The Faradays were a deeply religious family. Michael's parents had met and married in the Sandemanian Church at Kirkby Stephen in Westmorland. After moving down to London they regularly went to the small Sandemanian chapel in the City, near St. Paul's. The Sandemanians were a small closely-knit sect, which had broken away from the Scottish Presbyterian Church early in the eighteenth century. Their services were simple and their aim was to follow the example of the Christian Church of New Testament times. The members were humble but seemed rather anti-social since they preferred to find their friends from among the members of the sect. They held strong religious beliefs but did not believe in forcing their views on others. They thought it wrong to save up money. There were no paid clergy; the members elected Elders who took the services.

This was the community in which Michael Faraday grew up as a boy. He attended the little chapel whenever he could throughout his life, and it was there that he met his future wife, Sarah Barnard, the daughter of a silversmith. They were married in 1821. It was a happy marriage and they were well suited to each other. They had no children of their own, but their nieces were frequent and welcome visitors. Sarah was no intellectual, and she was happy to care for her husband without understanding his work. Faraday, too, did not feel any need to discuss his work with his wife or with anyone else. He was a solitary worker; Sergeant Anderson, who had come to help with the glass research, remained with Faraday for the rest of his life, and was the only assistant Faraday ever had.

Faraday kept his religion, his science and his do-

Right Faraday and his wife, Sarah.

Below Queen Victoria in 1841.

mestic life quite separate. A month after the marriage he formally joined the Church of which his wife was already a member, and in 1840 he was elected an Elder. His sermons, when he was called upon to preach, were earnest and dull, quite unlike his lively scientific lectures. But Faraday reading the Bible in Church was different again. A man who often listened to him found it "one of the richest treats that it has been my good fortune to enjoy."

Faraday once found himself subject to the strict discipline of his Church; he was deprived of his Elder-ship and even excluded from membership for a time. His offence was that he had been absent one Sunday without a good enough reason. In fact, he had been invited to dine with Queen Victoria at Windsor! However, in 1860 he returned to the Eldership.

Faraday's religion was a very personal matter, rarely mentioned in public. He did mention it in a lecture on education in 1854, but only to say that religious and scientific belief were two different things, and that the reason one applied to science could not be applied to religion. Still, it seems likely that his religious belief in a single Creator encouraged his scientific belief in the "unity of forces," the idea that magnetism, electricity and other forces have a common origin.

Faraday's way of life was very simple. After about 1834 he rarely went out to dinners and parties. It was not because he disapproved of such things; he pre-ferred to spend his time on scientific research. His income from the Royal Institution was not high com-pared with the earnings of other scientists. But it was a good income, and by taking on more consulting work he could have become a rich man. Much of his income went on charity. He often visited the poorer members of his Church, helping the needy with his own money.

He was a gentle man, but could be roused to anger. The Government sometimes awarded eminent men "pensions," annual sums of money to help them carry on work of public interest. In 1835 the Prime Minister, Viscount Melbourne, asked Faraday to call on him because the Government wanted to give him such a pension. In the conversation, Melbourne called the giving of pensions humbug. Faraday promptly left the interview, and wrote to Lord Melbourne declining the offer. However, Faraday's friends would not let the matter end like this. The affair was reported in *The Times*. The result was that the King himself intervened, Melbourne apologized, and Faraday received a pension of £300 per year for the rest of his life.

In 1825 the Managers of the Royal Institution wanted to show their appreciation of Faraday's work.

Right The programme of Faraday's first course of Christmas Lectures in 1827/8.

Royal Institution of Great Britain,

ALBEMARLE STREET,

December 3, 1827

A

COURSE OF SIX ELEMENTARY LECTURES

ON

CHEMISTRY,

ADAPTED TO A JUVENILE AUDIENCE, WILL BE DELIVERED
DURING THE CHRISTMAS RECESS,

BY MICHAEL FARADAY, F.R.S.

Corr. Mem. Royal Acad. Sciences, Paris; Director of the Laboratory, &c. &c.

The Lectures will commence at Three o'Clock.

Lecture I. Saturday, December 29. Substances generally—Solids, Fluids, Gases—Chemical affinity.

Lecture II. Tuesday, January 1, 1828. Atmospheric Air and its Gases.

Lecture III. Thursday, January 3. Water and its Elements.

Lecture IV. Saturday, January 5. Nitric Acid or Aquafortis—Ammonia or Volatile Alkali—Muriatic Acid or Spirit of Salt—Chlorine, &c.

Lecture V. Tuesday, January 8. Sulphur, Phosphorus, Carbon, and their Acids.

Lecture VI. Thursday, January 10. Metals and their Oxides—Earths, Fixed Alkalies and Salts, &c.

Non-Subscribers to the Institution are admitted to the above Course on payment of One Guinea each; Children 10s. 6d.

[Turn over.

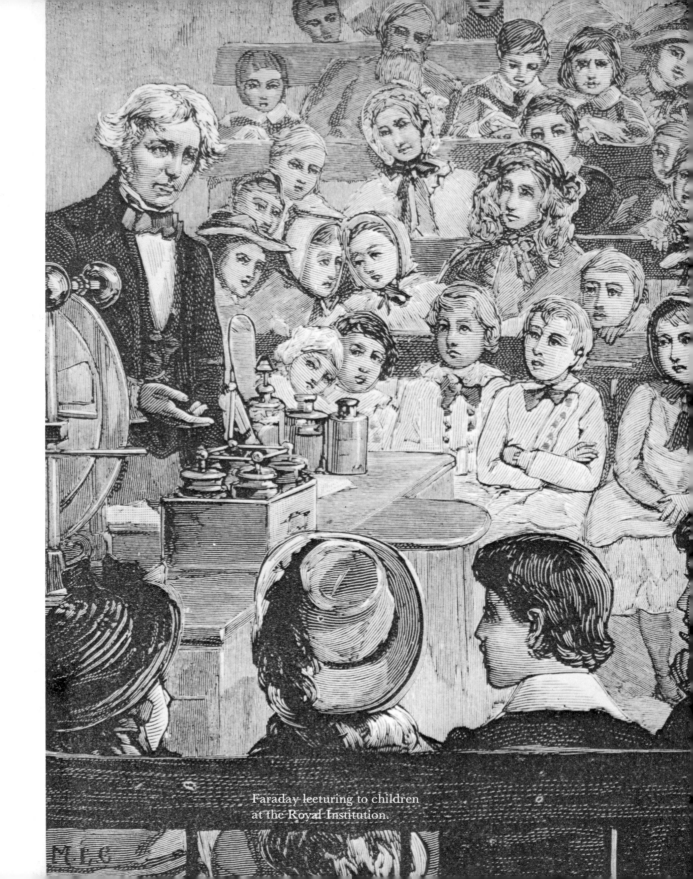
Faraday lecturing to children
at the Royal Institution.

They could not afford to raise his salary, but at Sir Humphry Davy's suggestion they appointed him Director of the Laboratory. In this new position, Faraday began two new activities in the Institution's programme: the first was a weekly evening meeting of members, and the second a series of lectures for children at Christmas.

The weekly meeting developed into the Friday Evening Discourses, which are still held today. The speaker is always a person of eminence, and the subject is usually scientific. The members and their guests meet in the theatre of the Royal Institution. At 9 p.m. precisely the clock strikes. The speaker enters, and begins his address without any introduction by the chairman. The lecture is often accompanied by slides and experimental demonstrations, and lasts one hour. Faraday himself gave many of the first Friday Evening Discourses, and he also gave several series of the Children's Christmas Lectures. These still continue and have been televised in recent years.

In 1833 a wealthy member of the Royal Institution, John Fuller, gave a sum of money to endow a professorship. Fuller stipulated that Faraday was to be the first Fullerian Professor of Chemistry. This raised Faraday's income from the Institution to £200 per year, at which it remained until 1853 when it became £300, after he was appointed "Superintendent of the House and Laboratories."

Lectures for children by leading scientists are still given at the Royal Institution. Here, Sir Lawrence Bragg, famous for his work on X-rays and crystals, is seen lecturing to children in 1962.

6 Electromagnetic Rotations

Faraday's first electrical discovery was made in 1821, when he had put aside his chemical work for a time. In the previous October he had read of an important discovery by the Danish scientist, Hans Christian Oersted. Oersted had found that an electric current flowing through a wire produced a magnetic effect. If the wire was held above a compass needle, the needle would turn at right angles to the wire when the current flowed. If the wire was held under the compass, but with the current still flowing in the same direction, then the needle turned the other way.

Before Oersted's discovery many people, including Faraday, believed that there must be some link between electricity and magnetism. Now this was proved. The relationship was a strange one, however, which is probably why it had not been found sooner. The force between two magnets tends either to bring them together, or to push them apart. The force between electrically charged objects behaves in a similar way, and the force of gravity always tends to

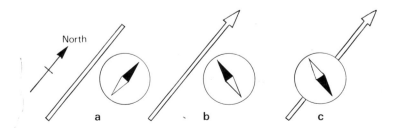

Fig. 2 Oersted's discovery—the effect of an electric current on a compass.
  (a) No current. Compass points North.
  (b) Current in the wire. Compass is deflected.
  (c) The current is still flowing in the same direction, but the wire is now placed *under* the compass. Compass is deflected in the opposite direction.

bring objects together. These are all called "central forces" because they act between one centre and another. But the current in Oersted's wire did not pull the compass needle towards the wire, nor did it push it away. Instead the current produced a mag-

Hans Christian Oersted
(1777–1851), the Danish
physicist who discovered in 1820
the magnetic effect produced by
an electric current.

netic force which seemed to act in a circle around the wire. It caused a sensation, and every scientist who read Oersted's paper tried the experiment for himself. The phenomenon was named "electromagnetism."

Two main ideas were suggested to explain electromagnetism. Some scientists thought that the wire carrying an electric current must itself become a magnet, and that electromagnetism was the interaction of two magnets—the compass needle and the wire. The Austrian J. J. Prechtl explained it in this way by suggesting that wire carrying an electric current became magnetized so that all the left-hand side of the wire was one magnetic pole, and the right-hand side was the other pole. This explained why the compass needle was deflected above or below the wire. It was a reason which depended on central forces, not circular ones.

But it left open the question why the wire became magnetized in that particular way. The Frenchman A.-M. Ampère (after whom the "ampère" or "amp," the unit of electric current is named) took the other view. He saw everything in terms of electric currents. He said that every permanent magnet contained circulating electric currents, and he showed that there was a force between two parallel wires carrying a current.

In England W. H. Wollaston also tried to explain electromagnetism by the existence of circulating currents. But he said that it was the current in the wire which "circulated" and went along the wire in a helical path. Wollaston thought that, because of the circulating path of the current, a wire would tend to rotate on its own axis when a magnet was brought near. In April 1821 he and Davy tried to make a wire rotate in that way, but failed.

Faraday took no part in any of these speculations at that time, partly because he was busy making steel alloys for James Stodart (as well as courting Sarah Barnard), and partly because he was poor at mathe-

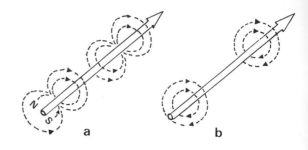

Fig. 3 The magnetic field around a wire carrying current,
(a) according to Prechtl's theory that the wire itself becomes a magnet.
(b) The actual arrangement of the lines of force.

matics. The various theories put forward were mostly mathematical and had little experimental basis. Later Faraday wrote to Ampère saying, "Your theory . . . so soon becomes mathematical that it quickly gets beyond my reach."

Not until the summer of 1821 did Faraday have time to follow up "electromagnetism" himself. He did so then because his friend Phillips, editor of the scientific journal *The Annals of Philosophy*, invited him to write an historical account of electromagnetism for the *Annals*. With his usual thoroughness, Faraday repeated all the important experiments of the other scientists while writing his account. As he studied the subject, he became convinced that it ought to be possible to produce continuous circular movement by making use of the circular magnetic force around a wire. In September 1821 he found how to do it. In

Faraday's study at the Royal Institution.

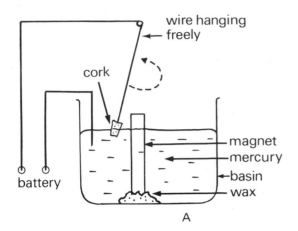

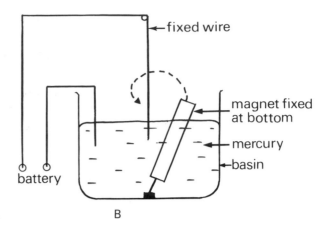

A

B

Fig. 4 Electromagnetic Rotations.
  (a) First method. The hanging
      wire rotates around the
      magnet.
  (b) Second method. The upper
      end of the magnet rotates
      around the fixed wire.
      (Note that the magnet
      floats in mercury.)

fact, he built two devices, really the first electric motors, to show "electromagnetic rotation."

In the first, he fixed a bar magnet vertically in a basin with a blob of wax. The basin was then nearly filled with mercury. A wire with a cork on its end was loosely fixed to a point above the basin, and a battery connected between the wire and another wire which dipped into the edge of the basin. "Very satisfactory," wrote Faraday in his notebook, after seeing the wire move in circles around the magnet.

In the second arrangement the magnet was fixed at the bottom, so that the upper end was free to move. The wire from above was fixed in the middle of the mercury. This way, the upper end of the magnet moves in circles around the fixed wire.

Faraday then had a special demonstration apparatus made which combined the rotating wire arrangement and the rotating magnet one; and he published an article on electromagnetic rotations in October. This apparatus was copied and the experiments repeated all over Europe. But Faraday's haste in announcing a discovery which brought him fame also created a most unpleasant situation.

It was well known that Wollaston had tried to make a wire revolve by electromagnetism; and at a quick glance Faraday's experiment was almost the same as Wollaston's. Faraday did not mention Wollaston's experiment when he published his own discovery, and many people thought at first that he had copied Wollaston's experiment without giving him credit. In fact, Faraday had been unable to contact Wollaston quickly, and did not like to quote his work without permission. Faraday's arrangement was really quite distinct from Wollaston's, but the incident caused much ill feeling just when Faraday was being proposed for Fellowship of the Royal Society. He was elected, but the decision was not unanimous. Sadly, it seems to have been Sir Humphry Davy who led the opposition to him.

7 Electricity from Magnetism

If an electric current could produce magnetic effects, could electricity be produced from magnetism? This was the question to which Faraday returned from time to time during the 1820s, but without success. He was inclined to accept Ampère's theory that magnetic effects were caused by electric currents, and he thought that if two wires were placed side by side and a current made to flow in one wire then some electric effect should be produced in the other.

In 1825 Faraday took two pieces of wire five feet

Lines of magnetic force as shown by iron filings sprinkled onto a sheet of paper under which a horseshoe magnet has been placed.

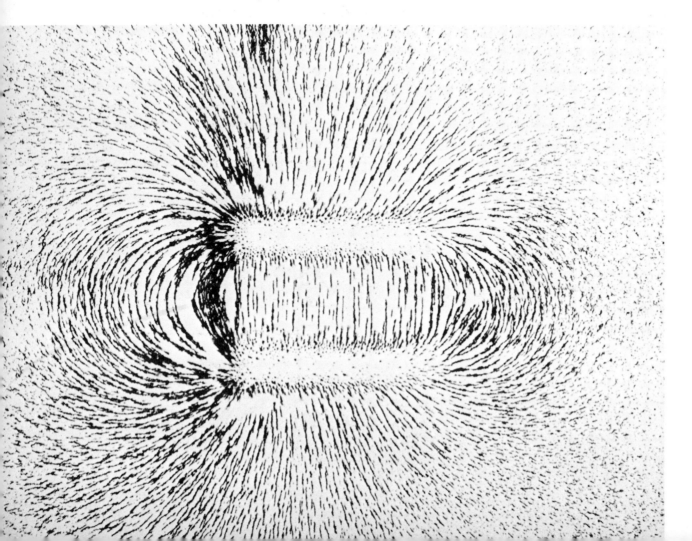

long, tied them together with just a single thickness of paper between them, and connected one to a battery. A galvanometer was connected to the other wire, but it showed nothing. Faraday continued with his research on glass.

The Frenchman Arago made an important discovery in 1824; he found that there was a force between a magnet and a moving copper plate. Arago had acquired a new compass, and he noticed that it was heavily damped; in other words, instead of oscillating violently and gradually settling down, the needle came to rest quite quickly in its final position. He investigated and found that this was because the compass had a copper base. If a fixed copper base tended to discourage movement of the needle, what would a moving one do? Arago pivoted a compass needle over a copper disc and made the disc go round. He found that the compass needle also went round, in the same direction as the disc. Subsequently it was found that if a magnet is rotated close to an electrically conducting disc then the disc tends to follow the magnet, and also that the effect is lessened if radial slits are cut in the plate.

These discoveries proved important when, in 1831, Faraday again turned from chemistry to electricity. For they suggested that the effect was due to electricity being produced in some way in the disc.

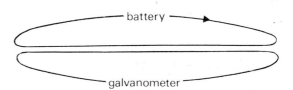

Fig. 5 Faraday's experiment of 1825. He hoped that the current in the upper wire would produce an effect in the lower one.

8 Electromagnetic Induction

The statue of Michael Faraday in the Royal Institution shows him holding a small piece of apparatus in his left hand. This is his "induction ring," with which he made one of the greatest of his discoveries on 29th August 1831. The discovery was electromagnetic induction: the induction (or generation) of electricity in a wire by means of the electromagnetic effect of a current in another wire. The section in Faraday's notebook is headed "Expts on the production of Electricity from Magnetism &c." It describes the first of a series of brilliant discoveries made during the autumn of 1831, which form the basis of modern electrical technology. The induction ring was the first electric transformer. A later discovery in the series was the first generator.

The induction ring is a simple device. Faraday wound two coils of wire on a ring of soft iron just under an inch thick and six inches in diameter. As the only wire made then was bare metal, he wound a piece of calico under each layer of wire and a piece of fine string between the turns. In that way each part of the wire was insulated both from the iron ring and from the adjacent turns. Each coil was wound in several parts, with both ends of each part brought out. This allowed him to use either the whole coil or just a part of it. He connected one coil (which he called "B") to a piece of wire which passed over a compass three feet away from the ring. After describ-

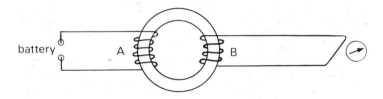

Fig. 6 The principle of Faraday's induction ring.

ing the ring and windings, Faraday wrote that he then "connected the ends of one of the pieces on A side with battery. Immediately a sensible effect on needle. It oscillated and settled at last in original position. On *breaking* connection of A side with Battery again a disturbance of the needle."

There was an effect in coil B when a current began

Statue of Faraday at the Royal Institution. He holds the induction ring in his hand.

to flow in coil A. This was "electromagnetic induction," the induction of electricity by means of electromagnetism. With more tests, he found that iron did not have to be used. He could show the effect with two coils wound on a cardboard tube, though it was much greater when the iron core was there.

When the experiment was made without the iron core, it was very like the 1825 experiment. Faraday had tied together two pieces of wire, connected the first one to a battery and looked for an indication on a galvanometer connected to the second. Why, therefore, did he fail to find the effect in 1825? His apparatus had probably been improved by 1831, but his understanding had also changed. In 1825 he expected the mere presence of a current in the first wire to produce an effect in the second. By 1831 he expected a new factor to be involved. This new factor was a movement or a change in something. He expected an effect in the second coil at the moment he completed the circuit of the first coil and battery. At that moment the current in the first coil changed, from nothing to something, and because he was looking for an effect then he found it. The compass needle swung to one side, oscillated to and fro, and finally settled in its original position. When the circuit of the first coil was broken, so that the current changed back to nothing, there was a similar effect; but the compass needle moved first in the opposite direction.

The discovery of electromagnetic induction was important for Faraday. He had been searching for some such effect on and off for ten years, and it helped his theoretical understanding of electricity and magnetism. The discovery is important to us for another reason. The induction ring was the first electric transformer, and the electricity supply industry is totally dependent on transformers.

Electric current may be either *alternating* (a.c.) or *direct* (d.c.). A torch battery produces direct current; it flows steadily in the same direction for as long as the torch is switched on. The electricity supplied to homes and factories by the electricity boards is alternating current; it flows first one way and then the other, alternately. In Britain there are fifty "cycles" or pulses of electricity in each direction, every second. In America the figure is sixty. With a suitable instrument, such as an oscilloscope, one can see how the pressure (or "voltage") of the electricity supply varies during the cycle. In fact, the pressure is always changing. If coil A of Faraday's induction ring were linked to the ordinary electricity supply there would be a current in it which was always changing, and so electricity would constantly be induced in coil B.

If the "waveform" (the shape of the curve in the illustration) of the current in coil A is arranged to be the curve known to mathematicians as a sine-wave, then the current induced in coil B has the same waveform. If the coils A and B have the same number of turns, the pressure in the circuit of coil B will be about the same as coil A. If B has more or less turns than A, then the pressure in its circuit will be more, or less, in proportion to the number of turns.

The generators in power stations work most efficiently if they are designed to generate electricity at a much higher pressure than is safe for domestic use. Sending electrical energy over many miles needs even higher pressures, to be done economically. So the pressure has to be changed several times between the generator and the customer. All these changes of pressure are made by transformers, which are basically iron cores with two coils of wire wound on them. Michael Faraday did not live to see a public electricity supply, but his induction ring, in a much larger form, is an essential element in the supply system today.

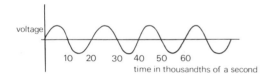

Fig. 7 The waveform of the ordinary (alternating current) electricity supply.

9 *Magneto-electric Induction*

Faraday's discovery of electromagnetic induction was put in his notebook under the heading "Expts on the production of Electricity from Magnetism &c." But he had not produced electricity from magnetism. This he sought to do in the following weeks.

He gathered together a variety of coils of wire, magnets and pieces of iron. Success came on 2nd September 1831, when he was experimenting with two bar magnets and a cylindrical coil wound on an iron bar. The two magnets and the iron bar were arranged in a triangular manner to form a complete "magnetic circuit," and the coil was connected to a galvanometer. When the magnetic circuit was broken, by removing the iron bar, the galvanometer showed a brief electric current. On putting the iron bar back a brief current flowed the opposite way. This was undoubtedly magnetism being converted into electricity. Faraday called it magneto-electric induction (the induction of electricity by means of a magnet) to distinguish it from his earlier discovery of electromagnetic induction.

In October of the same year Faraday found another way of arranging his coils and magnets to produce magneto-electric induction. Using a coil wound on a hollow paper cylinder he found that electricity was induced in the coil if a bar magnet was either thrust quickly into the coil, or pulled quickly out.

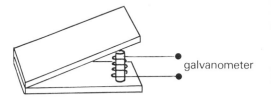

Fig. 8 *Above* Magneto-electric induction—first method.
The coil of wire wound on a short iron rod is placed as shown between two bar magnets. When the coil is pulled out (or the two magnets pulled apart) the galvanometer indicates that a brief current flows.

Right The entry in Faraday's diary recording the discovery of electromagnetic induction.

Fig. 9 *Left* Magneto-electric induction—second method.
As the bar magnet is thrust into the wire coil which is wound on a paper tube, the galvanometer shows that a brief current flows. As the magnet is withdrawn, the current flows in the opposite direction.

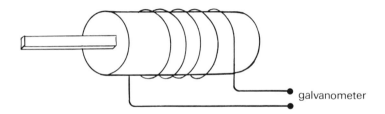

Aug. 29th 1831.

Expts on the production of Electricity from Magnetism &c

2   Have had an iron ring made (soft iron), iron round about 1 inch
thick & ring 6 inches in external diameter   Wound many
coils of copper wire round one half the coils being separated
by twine & calico – there were 3 lengths of wire each about 24
feet long and they could be connected as one length or used
as separate lengths   By trial with a trough each was
insulated from the other.   Will call this side of the ring
A.   On the other side but separated by an
interval was wound wire in two pieces
together amounting to about 60 feet in
length the direction being as with the former
coils   this side call B.

        Charged a battery of 10 pr plates 4 inches square   Made
the coil on B side one coil and connected its extremities by
a copper wire passing to a distance and put over a magnetic
needle (3 feet from wire ring)   Then connected the end of one of the
pieces on A side with battery   immediately a sensible effect on needle
It oscillated & settled at last in original position.   On breaking
connection of A side with Battery again a disturbance
of the needle

        Made all the wires on A side one coil and sent cur-
rent from battery through the whole.   Effect on needle much
stronger than before –

        The effect on the needle then but a very small part of
that which the wire communicating directly with the battery
could produce

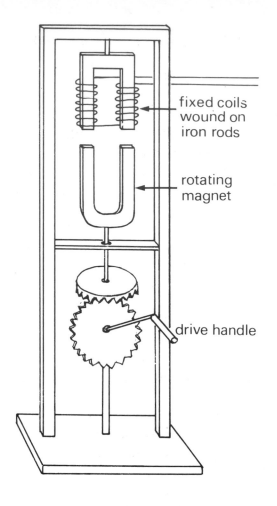

fixed coils
wound on
iron rods

rotating
magnet

drive handle

Fig. 10 *Left, and right* Pixii's machine which produces an alternating electric current in its coils as the magnet rotates.

When this fact became known several scientists, though apparently not Faraday, made hand-operated generators in which either a magnet was moved to and fro inside a fixed coil, or a coil was moved to and fro in front of a permanent magnet. The modern electric generator uses *rotary* motion between the magnet and the coil, rather than a to-and-fro motion in a straight line. The first such generator was made in Paris by a young French instrument maker, Hippolyte Pixii. All the generators in power stations today have grown from the machine Pixii made after reading of Faraday's discoveries.

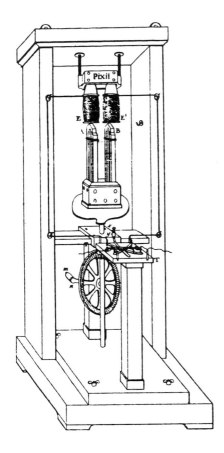

Faraday did make a generator himself, but it was quite different from Pixii's. Pixii's machine produced alternating current as the coils passed from the north pole of the magnet to the south pole and then back to the north pole again. For public electricity supply the alternating current output is ideal, because it allows transformers to be used as already explained.

Faraday wanted a machine which would produce a steady direct current, like a battery. For that he needed to make a conductor move *continuously in the same direction* past the poles of a magnet. That may sound impossible, but it can be done if the conductor is part of a rotating copper disc. He arranged the disc to spin between the poles of a large permanent magnet and made two sliding connections with pieces of springy metal. One connection was on the axis, and the other on the edge of the disc near the magnet. While the disc was moving, electricity was induced in the part of the disc between the sliding contacts. In this way a continuous output was obtained. Faraday's "disc generator" is of little practical use, but it showed how much he had learned about electricity and magnetism. It also enabled him to explain Arago's discovery that a copper plate would damp down the oscillations of a compass. The movement of the compass magnet generated electric currents in the disc, and these in turn produced a magnetic field which acted on the compass to oppose its movement.

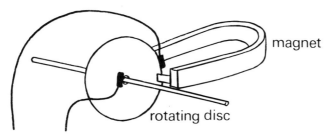

wires to sliding contacts pressing on disc

Fig. 11 Faraday's disc generator.

10 *Many Electricities—or One?*

In August 1832, Faraday began another series of electrical researches. This time he was not trying to find new effects, but to show that all kinds of electricity were in fact forms of the same thing. Although he thought that the electricity he had produced from a magnet by induction was the same as volta-electricity (electricity from a battery), and that both were the same as static electricity, he had not actually proved it. Having made the disc generator, which produced a continuous current of magneto-electricity, it was easy to show that magneto-electricity and volta-electricity produced the same effects.

The current from both sources would heat a fine wire, produce magnetism, and cause chemical decomposition when passed through certain liquids, including water. It was much harder to show that static electricity was the same. Magneto-electricity and volta-electricity were characterized by their heating, magnetic and chemical effects. But static electricity involved the attraction and repulsion of charged bodies and the production of sparks. Could these two "electricities" really be the same?

Faraday realized that the apparent difference between the static electricity produced by his frictional machine, and the electricity from batteries and magneto devices, was that the static electricity was at a much higher "tension" or voltage. He proved that it could produce magnetic effects by connecting his frictional machine to a sensitive galvanometer by a wet thread. When the machine was turned the galvanometer needle moved.

For his first demonstration of chemical effects, his apparatus consisted of two silver wires dipped into a solution of copper sulphate. He knew that if an elec-

Cartoon from *Punch*, 27th June, 1891 commemorating the centenary of Faraday's birth.

A SCIENTIFIC CENTENARY.

Faraday (returned). "WELL, MISS SCIENCE, I HEARTILY CONGRATULATE YOU; YOU HAVE MADE MARVELLOUS PROGRESS SINCE MY TIME!"

tric current from a battery were passed from one wire to the other through the solution, then one wire would become plated with copper. He fixed one silver wire to his frictional machine and the other to earth. After about a hundred turns of the machine he found a deposit of copper on one of the wires. So static electricity could indeed produce chemical effects.

It had been known for years that volta-electricity could produce sparks; Humphry Davy had shown

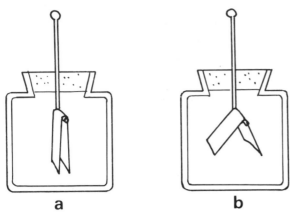

Electroscope (a) not charged
(b) charged

Fig. 12 Gold-leaf electroscope, (a) not charged, (b) charged. Two pieces of gold-leaf hang from a metal support. When there is no electric charge present they hang together. If an electric charge is put on the instrument, both leaves become charged and repel each other.

that before Faraday went to the Royal Institution. Faraday himself had shown that his magneto-electricity could produce a small spark, though the experiment proved difficult because the spark was so feeble.

The force between bodies charged with static electricity is best seen with an electroscope. In this device two pieces of gold leaf are suspended on a piece of metal fixed in the top of a glass jar. When the charge from a frictional electric machine is passed to the metal, the gold leaves become charged with the same polarity, and so repel each other. Faraday showed that the current from a battery could also charge the electroscope. In other words, static electricity and voltaic and magneto-electricity all produced similar effects. There was only one type of electricity, not two or three.

There were two other sources of "electricities" which Faraday studied in an effort to show that they also were the same. One was "thermo-electricity" and the other "animal electricity." Despite many trials, he was unable to prove that the shock given by various electric fishes, such as the torpedo, was caused by the same kind of electricity. But he was convinced that it must be so. Some of these trials were made with the help of his friend Professor Wheatstone. The entries in Faraday's diary are brief, and we cannot tell how he set about getting electricity from the fish. Once he wrote, "Tried Mr. Wheatstone's apparatus. It did not do." Alas, Faraday did not say what "it" was or what it did not do—but it is comforting for modern students to know that even Faraday's experiments sometimes failed completely!

Faraday had more success with thermo-electricity. If two different metals are joined into a circuit—with one junction kept cold, the other heated—current will flow. But the voltage is so small that it is very hard to produce a spark. Faraday did not see a "thermo-electric spark" until 1837, when he met with Wheatstone and the American Professors Henry and Bache in Wheatstone's laboratory at King's College London. It was Professor Henry's apparatus which finally produced the spark, and when he saw it Faraday jumped up with excitement, shouting, "Hurrah for the Yankee experiment!"

11 *Electrochemistry*

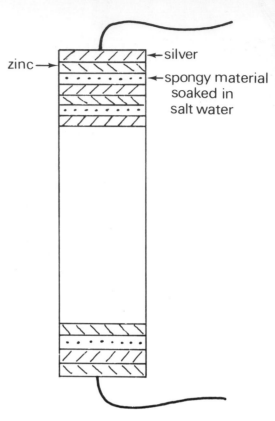

Faraday had used chemical effect as one of the tests to show that electricity was the same, wherever it came from. He went on to study the whole subject of "electrochemistry" and worked out the general scientific laws which apply to chemical reactions produced by electricity.

Water breaks down into hydrogen and oxygen when an electric current passes through it. This fact was demonstrated in 1800 only a few months after the Italian scientist Alessandro Volta made his "pile." Volta's pile was the first electric battery, the first source of a continuous electric current. It consisted of a pile of pairs of plates or discs of two different metals (Volta preferred silver and zinc). These were interleaved with pieces of spongy material such as cloth or cardboard soaked in salt water. Among the many scientists who quickly made their own pile were two Englishmen, William Nicholson and Anthony Carlisle. Nicholson was a chemist and also editor of a scientific journal; Carlisle was a surgeon. Their pile consisted of seventeen silver coins and the same number of discs of copper and pieces of cloth soaked in salt water. When wires connected to the two ends of the pile were dipped in a vessel of water, they found that gas was given off at each wire. On collecting the gases they found that it was hydrogen given off at the negative wire, and oxygen at the positive one. The volume of the hydrogen was twice the volume of the oxygen, and they correctly deduced that they had decomposed some of the water into its elements. This process became known as "electrolysis."

It was soon found that a variety of substances could be decomposed if they were first dissolved in water, and an electric current then passed through the solu-

Fig. 13 *Above* Volta's pile.

Fig. 14 *Below* The electrolysis of water. (A little acid is added to increase the water's electrical conductivity. Faraday used platinum wires, for if copper is used, some of the oxygen will react with it, and the two gases will not be collected in the ratio 2 : 1.)

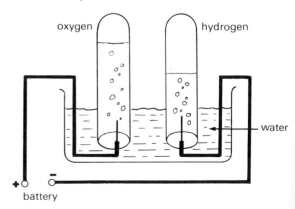

Above The Voltaic pile which Alessandro Volta (1745–1827) presented to Faraday.

Fig. 15 *Below* Electroplating.

tion. If copper sulphate was used it was found that pure copper metal was deposited on the positive wire. This led to the new industry of electroplating, in which a coating of a more expensive metal such as silver is deposited on cutlery or other objects made of a cheaper metal, and connected to the positive wire of an electrochemical cell. In his early years at the Royal Institution, Humphry Davy made a study of electrochemistry, and obtained several previously unknown elements.

Faraday noticed that water will conduct electricity, but ice will not. He made a systematic study of substances which could be melted to find out how well they conducted in both the solid and liquid states. He found that metals always conduct electricity and fatty substances never do. Almost everything else conducted electricity when in its liquid form, but not when solid. The last group of substances were all compounds; when an electric current was passed through the substance in its melted state, chemical decomposition took place.

While studying the identity of electricity from different sources, Faraday made some measurements of quantity of electricity. He measured how much

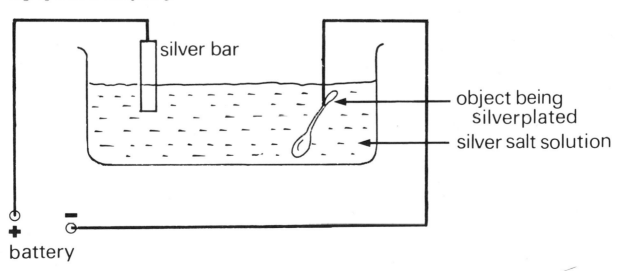

silver bar

object being silverplated
silver salt solution

battery

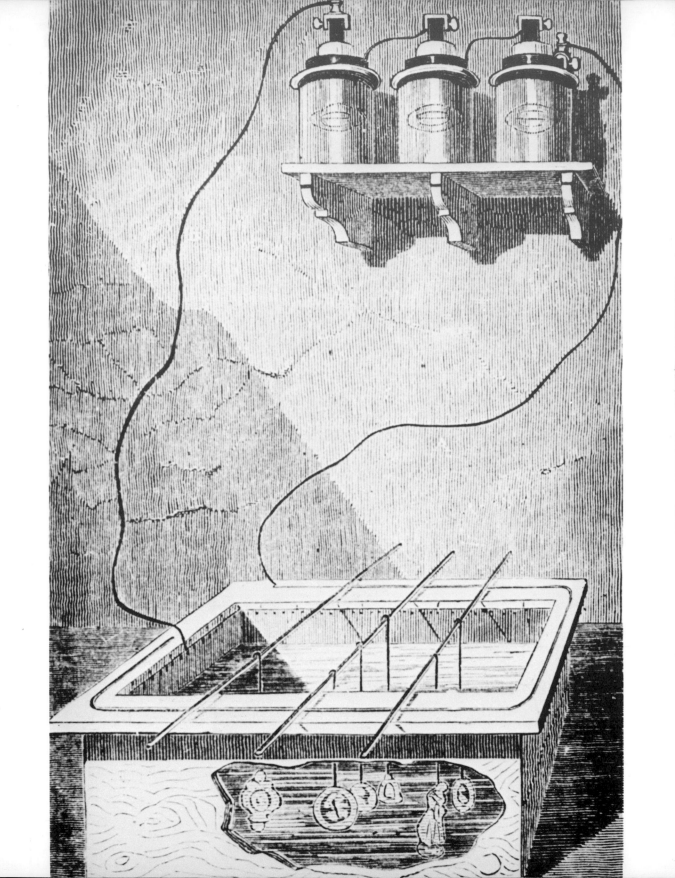

electricity came from a battery by timing the period for which it was connected; he said that the quantity of electricity which came from a frictional electric machine depended on the number of turns of the handle. He noted, for example, that the electric current from his battery during eight beats of his watch produced the same magnetic and chemical effects as the electricity from his frictional machine when the handle was turned round thirty times.

He now measured the quantity of chemical effect produced by a definite amount of electricity. If the chemical product was a gas he measured its volume; if it was a solid he weighed it. He found that the chemical effect was always in proportion to how much electricity flowed, whatever the size or shape of the apparatus. In his own words: "chemical action or decomposing power is exactly proportional to the quantity of electricity which passes." This is the First Law of Electrolysis. Every substance which can be discharged in an electrochemical process (such as hydrogen or oxygen in the electrolysis of water, or copper in copper plating) has an "electrochemical equivalent." This is the weight of substance given off when a standard quantity of electricity passes through the electrochemical cell.

Faraday made an instrument for measuring quantity of electricity, based on the first law. He called it the "volta electrometer" because it was a meter for measuring electricity from a Volta's pile. The name was soon shortened to "voltameter." In its simplest form, it was a glass tube in which two platinum wires were fixed. The tube was filled with water containing a little acid to increase its electrical conductivity.

To measure the quantity of electricity flowing in a circuit, the volta electrometer was included in the circuit. As the current flowed the water was electrolysed, yielding oxygen and hydrogen gases; the volume of the gas could be read on a scale on the side of the tube.

Electroplating apparatus of the late 1860s.

63

The volume of gas was directly proportional to the quantity of electricity which had passed. So, if another electrochemical cell was put in the circuit, Faraday could measure with the volta electrometer how much electricity passed through the other cell. In this way he measured the electrochemical equivalents of a great many substances. He established the Second Law of Electrolysis, which says that the electrochemical equivalent of a substance is proportional to its ordinary chemical equivalent. (The chemical equivalent of a substance is the number of grams of it which combines with eight grams of oxygen.)

When advances are made in any branch of science, new technical words and phrases often have to be invented. As Faraday went deeper into electrochemical action, he found he needed a number of new words, partly because he was describing new things but partly also because existing words were often associated in people's minds with old theories and ideas which Faraday himself did not accept. At this time most scientists still thought of electricity as an "imponderable fluid." Some looked on electrochemical reactions as processes in which the "electric fluid" formed chemical compounds with other substances. Faraday himself saw electricity as a force which acted on substances, rather than as a substance itself. To avoid misunderstanding, he decided to introduce a series of new words when, in January 1834, he published a paper setting out his discoveries in electrochemistry.

Faraday discussed the choice of words with a number of language experts, including the Rev. William Whewell, a Cambridge professor, who had devised several scientific words which remain in use today. Faraday was himself interested in words. Later, when the word *scientist* came into the English language in 1840, he wrote to Whewell saying he thought it a good word and asking Whewell to invent something better than *physicist* which, said Faraday,

Faraday's voltameter which he invented for measuring the amount of electricity flowing in an electric circuit.

E.U.Eidis delin.

eug.

W.O. 1810.

66

was "so awkward that I think I shall never be able to use it." In 1833 Faraday suggested a number of words which Whewell rejected, but in the end they agreed on a series of terms which remain in use today.

The liquid he called the *electrolyte*. The connections where the electric current entered and left the liquid he called *electrodes*. The *anode* was the electrode connected to the positive side of the battery, and the other was the *cathode*. The electrolyte, or the part of it which was decomposed, divided into two *ions*; the ions which went to the anode were called *anions* and the others *cations*.

When water is decomposed the water itself is the *electrolyte*; the *anion* is oxygen and the *cation* is hydrogen. In electroplating the object being plated forms the *cathode* and the *cation* is the metal being deposited.

William Whewell (1794–1866), the Master of Trinity College, Cambridge, who helped Faraday choose new words to describe the new ideas that he was introducing.

12 *Faraday's Later Scientific Work*

In 1835, after several years of continuous hard work, Faraday was in need of a holiday. He made a tour of Switzerland during which he renewed his friendship with the Swiss scientists, the father and son, G. and A. de la Rive, and then returned to the Royal Institution to carry on his research work. By 1838 his health was failing and he had to do less work.

In 1841 he needed a complete rest. He left the Royal Institution for eight months during which he again went to Switzerland with his wife and her brother. For the rest of his life he suffered loss of memory and attacks of giddiness, though his physical health was mostly good. During the winter of 1849–50 he was troubled by a persistent sore throat which prevented him from lecturing. The trouble was traced to some bad teeth which were later extracted. Michael Faraday's account of going to the dentist shows how fair-minded he was, even in a matter which had brought him great pain: "Because of much pain in my jaw and the known bad state of my teeth . . . I went on Monday morning to the dentist. He pulled out five teeth and a fang. He had much trouble and I much pain . . . On the whole the operation was well and cleverly carried on by the dentist, the fault was in the teeth."

His later work was a series of short bursts of activity rather than the long periods of research which had filled his earlier years. His memory often failed him when he tried to recall recent events, but he could recall events of long before, including the unfortunate incident in 1821 when he was suspected of stealing Wollaston's ideas. He was reluctant to begin research into subjects on which other people were working, in case the same thing happened again. Much of his time now was spent on advising the Government and other public bodies on scientific matters (see next chapter).

When Faraday went back to work towards the end of 1835, the subject he chose to study was static electricity or, as it was usually called then, "common electricity." He soon showed that when a body received an electric charge an equal but opposite charge appeared on neighbouring bodies. If the charged body is itself a conductor of electricity, then the charge spreads over the outer surface.

In a dramatic experiment he had a large wooden

The Library of the Royal Institution in 1809.

cage covered with conducting material built in the middle of the lecture theatre. The cage was insulated from the floor and connected to a frictional electric machine. Faraday's assistant then charged up the cage so that sparks flew from it. Meanwhile Faraday, sitting inside the cage, found that even with his most delicate apparatus he could detect no electric effects. Whatever it was that happened when a body was charged, it took place in the space between the surface of the body and its surroundings.

He decided to examine the space, and to do this had two sets of apparatus made consisting of two concentric spheres. The outer sphere could be opened so that the insulating material in the space could be changed. If the two sets of apparatus were connected and charged by a frictional electric machine, the "tension" or voltage between the inner and outer spheres would be the same. If the two devices were then disconnected and connected separately to a gold-leaf electroscope, each would produce the same deflection of the leaves. But when Faraday made the experiment again with *different* materials in the two spaces, he found that the two devices produced different deflections of the leaves. So the quantity of electric charge on the two devices somehow depended upon the insulating substance. The relationship between the charge and the tension he called the "specific inductive capacity" of the substance. This relationship is now known as the dielectric constant.

These experiments showed that something happened in an insulating material which was subjected to electric forces. Faraday made a search for some other evidence of that something. He found two effects which he could not explain, but which helped the advance of physical science and are known by his name. They are "Faraday's dark space" and the "Faraday effect."

The "dark space" was found when he examined electric discharges in air. The apparatus he used for

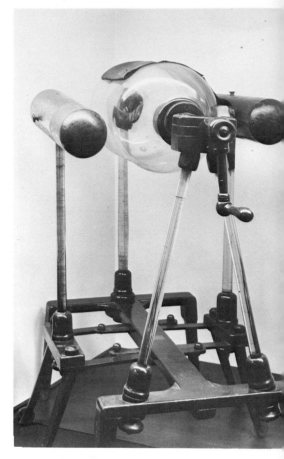

A frictional electric machine of the type used by Faraday to investigate the nature of electrically charged matter. This particular machine, in use throughout much of Faraday's lifetime, was built in 1803.

The "electric egg" used by Faraday to study electrical discharges in gases at different pressures.

this, which he called the "electric egg," consisted of an egg-shaped glass bulb with two metal balls mounted inside. With an air pump the pressure inside could be reduced to a very small value, and the metal balls were connected to a source of electricity. Faraday found that, if the electric tension was high enough, there was a luminous discharge between the two balls. However, under certain conditions, the discharge was not continuous from one ball to the other, but was broken near the cathode (the ball connected to the negative side of the source) by a dark region. He could not explain the effect, but he recorded carefully what he saw.

Faraday believed that there must be some basic connection between all the forces of nature. It had been shown that there was a close connection between electricity and magnetism, and by 1845 he was convinced that they must be connected in some way with light. In that year, he found the "Faraday effect." This occurs when polarized light passes through a suitable transparent material in the presence of a magnetic field. Polarized light is light in which the vibrations are all (or mostly) in the same plane, and the transparent material in which he found the effect was a piece of heavy glass he had made for the Royal Society about twenty years earlier. Faraday found that when no magnet was present the light passed through the glass unchanged. But when a powerful magnet was brought near the glass, the plane of polarization was turned.

This experiment suggested to Faraday that a powerful magnet might have *some* effect on the glass, even though glass is not magnetic. He suspended a piece of glass very delicately between the poles of a large horse-shoe electromagnet, and found that the glass tended to turn across the magnetic lines of force (a piece of magnetic material would have tended to turn so as to lie along the magnetic lines of force). He called the new phenomenon "diamagnetism."

After testing many substances he found that most things are diamagnetic, though a few non-magnetic substances tend to set themselves along the lines of force. These are called "paramagnetic."

Faraday made no more major scientific discoveries, though he tried to find a link between gravity and electricity by searching for electrical effects in falling bodies. His last experiment, in 1862, was to look for a change in the wavelength of light when passed through a strong magnetic field. He did not find any change: his ideas were right but his apparatus was not sensitive enough. The effect is now known as the Zeeman effect after the Dutch physicist Pieter Zeeman who found it in 1896.

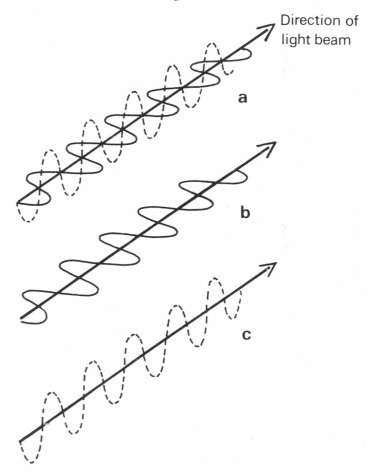

Direction of light beam

a

b

c

Left This dark, old photograph showing Faraday with J. F. Daniell in 1841 was taken in the very early days of photography, just six years after W. H. Fox Talbot had produced the first camera pictures on paper. J. F. Daniell (1790–1845), was Professor of Chemistry at King's College London, and known for the Daniell Cell.

Fig. 16 *Right* The polarization of light.
(a) Ordinary light has vibration in all directions. Some transparent substances will let through only the vibrations in a particular direction.
(b) Polarized light. This diagram represents a horizontally polarized beam of light.
(c) A vertically polarized beam of light.

13 *A Public Figure*

Faraday was now a public figure whose advice was sought by the Government on important scientific matters. For many years he had declined to act as a consultant because he wanted to spend all his time and energy on research. One of his last pieces of consultancy had been in 1832 for the Admiralty, when he analysed some samples of oatmeal which were suspected of being adulterated. Now that his health stopped him doing continuous research, his talents were again available to the Government.

In 1844 there was a public outcry about the safety of coal mines after ninety-five miners were killed in an explosion at Haswell Colliery in County Durham. The Prime Minister, Sir Robert Peel, decided that a chemist and a geologist should make an inquiry into the accident to find the cause, and recommend ways of avoiding similar accidents in future. Faraday and Sir Charles Lyell were chosen and travelled to Durham to hold their inquiry. They found that it was possible to light a pipe from a Davy safety lamp, and that although smoking was strictly forbidden there had been cases of men smoking in the mine.

Lyell noticed with surprise how Faraday changed from a scientific investigator into an able cross-examiner. Faraday had taken a keen interest in the question of the reliability of evidence. In one of his notebooks he compared the values of evidence and argument: "Testimony is like an arrow shot from a longbow; the force of it depends on the strength of the hand that draws it. Argument is like an arrow shot from a crossbow, which has equal force though shot by a child."

During the inquiry Faraday asked one of the mine inspectors how they measured the rate at which air

Sir Charles Lyell (1797–1875), the geologist who accompanied Faraday to conduct an inquiry into the disaster at Haswell Colliery in 1844 in which ninety-five miners were killed in an explosion.

flowed through the mine. The inspector showed how it was done. He took a pinch of gunpowder in one hand and a lighted candle in the other. The gunpowder was allowed to fall through the candle flame, and an assistant with a watch noted how long the smoke took to travel a certain distance. Faraday asked where the gunpowder was kept. The inspector seemed reluctant to tell him, but said it was kept in a bag whose neck was tied up. "But where do you keep the bag?" demanded Faraday. "You are sitting on it," came the reply. It was the most comfortable seat available, so they had given it to Faraday!

Faraday was one of a committee set up in 1850 to look into the problem of preserving the paintings in the National Gallery. London in those days was a dirty, smoky city, and the combined effects of dirt in the air and the close presence of thousands of visitors every day was wreaking havoc on the pictures. The committee recommended that all the pictures should be covered with glass, and this was done. It was appreciated that this was not a complete solution to the problem, and Faraday made a study of the chemistry of varnishes for covering pictures.

Later he was consulted about the famous Elgin marbles at the British Museum. He found, however, that nothing could be done to restore the marbles to their original condition, though he suggested ways of stopping further deterioration.

For nearly thirty years, until 1851, Faraday lectured in chemistry at the Royal Military Academy at Woolwich, and from 1836 he was a Scientific Adviser to Trinity House, the body which runs the lighthouses around the coast. The advisory post seems to have brought very little work until the later 1850s, when he had to advise on new ways of lighting lighthouses. The most promising proposal was for an electric light using an arc lamp and generator designed by a Professor Holmes. Faraday recommended that Holmes' scheme should be tried out in a light-

Left The Elgin marbles at the British Museum for which Faraday suggested methods of preservation, *and overpage* the Royal Military Academy, Woolwich, where Faraday lectured on chemistry for thirty years.

Trinity House, which runs the lighthouses around the coast, where Faraday was Scientific Adviser from 1836.

house, and this was done. His report to Trinity House was not only concerned with the question of whether Holmes' light would work, but also considered the cost of running the steam engine which drove the generator and the higher wages that would have to be paid for skilled men to operate the new equipment. When any new idea was being tried out in a lighthouse someone had to check that all was well. Even when he was seventy years old, Faraday still made occasional visits on behalf of Trinity House. In one report written in 1860 he explained that he had tried to visit a lighthouse but the road was blocked by snow. When he returned a few days later the road was still blocked, but he managed to cross walls, hedges and fields to reach the lighthouse and finish his work.

In 1862 Faraday gave evidence to the Public

Schools Commission. This was a Royal Commission set up with the Earl of Clarendon as chairman to investigate the education given in the Public Schools. Faraday drew the Commissioners' attention to the complete lack of science teaching in the Public Schools. He complained that people who had received the traditional Public School education based on the classics were ignorant of natural science and, what made it worse, they did not realize that they were ignorant. Faraday was asked whether science could be taught in such a way that examinations could be set to test the pupils. He was sure it was possible. He drew attention to the enthusiasm of schoolboys and girls who attended his lectures, and stressed the need for good teaching.

Apart from his own lifetime's experience of lecturing on scientific subjects, Faraday could also speak from his experience as a Senator of the University of London. The University had been established in 1836 as an examining body, not a teaching one, and one of the honours which gave Faraday most pleasure was his appointment by the Crown as one of the first members of the Senate.

14 *The Years of Retirement*

Queen Victoria's consort, Prince Albert, was interested in scientific matters and was largely responsible for the Great Exhibition of 1851. He had a high regard for Faraday, and took his son the Prince of Wales (later Edward VII) to hear him lecture. A painting of the scene by Alexander Blaikley now hangs in the Institution. Faraday himself was invited to Windsor Castle to discuss science with Prince Albert.

The "Crystal Palace" housing the Great Exhibition, which was opened by Queen Victoria on May 1st, 1851.

It was at Prince Albert's suggestion that in 1858 the Queen offered Faraday a Grace and Favour Residence, a house at Hampton Court for the rest of his life. Faraday hesitated to accept at first, for fear that he could not afford the cost of certain repairs. When this came to the Queen's ears she arranged for the repairs to be done at her own expense, and Faraday gladly accepted the house. Until 1862 he still spent most of his time at the Royal Institution, but thereafter Hampton Court became his home.

By 1861 Faraday knew that he could no longer carry out all his duties, especially the Juvenile Lectures for which he felt a clear and ordered mind was particularly essential. His letter of resignation includes his own account of how he first came to the Institution and how he felt about his work there.

Below The grace-and-favour house at Hampton Court given to Faraday by Queen Victoria for his retirement. He died there in 1867

Michael and Sarah,
Faraday, their niece Jane,
and John Tyndall
(1820-93), Professor of
Natural Philosophy at the
Royal Institution. This
photograph was taken in
about 1858.

Michael Faraday in
later life.

"To the Managers of the Royal Institution,
It is with the deepest feeling that I address you.
I entered the Royal Institution in March 1813,
nearly forty-nine years ago, and, with exception of
a comparatively short period, during which I was
abroad on the Continent with Sir H. Davy, have
been with you ever since. During that time I have
been most happy in your kindness, and in the fos-
tering care which the Royal Institution has be-
stowed upon me. Thank God, first, for all his gifts.

I have next to thank you and your predecessors for the unswerving encouragement and support which you have given me during that period. My life has been a happy one, and all that I desired. During its progress I have tried to make a fitting return for it to the Royal Institution, and through it to science. But the progress of years (now amounting in number to threescore and ten) having brought forth first the period of development, and then that of maturity, have ultimately produced for me that of gentle decay. This has taken place in such a manner as to make the evening of life a blessing; for whilst increasing physical weakness occurs, a full share of health free from pain is granted with it; and whilst memory and certain other faculties of the mind diminish, my good spirits and cheerfulness do not diminish with them.

Still I am not able to do as I have done . . ."

The Managers accepted his resignation as lecturer, but asked him to stay as Superintendent of the house and laboratories. These remaining duties he resigned in 1865, so ending all his connection with the Royal Institution. The feeling of the members towards him was such that the previous year he had been offered the Presidency of the Institution, but he declined because he knew he was no longer able to carry out the duties of this office.

In his last years, Michael Faraday gradually became weaker, and died peacefully sitting in his armchair at Hampton Court on 25th August 1867. By his own wish the funeral was private and simple, and the stone on his grave in Highgate cemetery recorded simply his name and the dates of his birth and death.

Date Chart

1791	Michael Faraday born 22nd September
1799	Royal Institution founded in London
1800	Volta's pile. Water decomposed by electricity
1801	Davy appointed to Royal Institution
1804	Faraday went to work for Riebau as an errand boy
1805	Faraday apprenticed to Riebau as a bookbinder
1810	Faraday joined the City Philosophical Society, London
1812	Faraday heard Davy lecture, completed his apprenticeship (7th October), and was introduced to Davy
1813	Appointed laboratory assistant at Royal Institution, 1st March. Began European Tour, 13th October
1814	Napoleon defeated and exiled to Elba
1815	Davy and Faraday returned to London, April. Faraday again employed by Royal Institution Battle of Waterloo, June, Napoleon's final defeat
1816	First scientific publication by Faraday, *Analysis of Native Caustic Lime of Tuscany*. Lectured to City Philosophical Society
1818–1823	Faraday's research on steel
1818 *onwards*	Faraday acting as a Consultant Chemist
1820	Oersted demonstrated the magnetic effect of an electric current. Death of George III, accession of George IV
1821	Faraday married Sarah Barnard. Joined Sandemanian Church. Made his first

	electrical discovery (electromagnetic rotations). Elected Fellow of the Royal Society
1823	Chlorine liquefied by Faraday
1824–1831	Faraday's research on glass
1824	Arago found force between a magnet and a rotating copper disc
1825	Analysis of benzene. Faraday appointed "Director of the Laboratory" and started the Friday Evening Discourses at the Royal Institution
1830	Accession of William IV
1831	Discovery of electromagnetic induction, August. Magneto-electric induction, September.
1832	Faraday sought to prove that electricity was always the same whatever its source
1833	Faraday appointed Fullerian Professor of Chemistry. Discovered Laws of Electrochemistry and devised new scientific words
1835	Holiday in Switzerland. Researches on static electricity. Awarded a pension
1836	London University established and Faraday appointed to the Senate
1837	Victoria became Queen. First practical electric telegraph
1840	Faraday became an Elder of his Church
1841	Faraday in poor health and in need of a complete rest. Spent eight months in Switzerland with his wife and her brother
1844	Faraday and Lyell conducted mining disaster inquiry
1845	The "Faraday effect" found
1851	The Great Exhibition, London
1850s	Faraday active as Scientific Consultant for the Government

1858	Queen Victoria gave Faraday a Grace and Favour house at Hampton Court
1861	Faraday resigned as Juvenile Lecturer
1862	Last scientific research. Gave evidence to the Public Schools Commission
1864	Declined the Presidency of the Royal Institution
1865	Resigned all remaining duties at the Royal Institution
1867	Faraday died 25th August
1881	The first public electricity supply (at Godalming, Surrey)

Glossary

ADULTERATED Mixed with poorer material

ALLOY A mixture of two or more metals

ANION An ion drawn towards the anode

ANODE Electrode connected to the positive side of a battery

ARC LAMP An electric light in which the light comes from a spark between two pieces of carbon

CALICO A cotton cloth from *Calicut* in India

CATHODE Electrode connected to the negative side of a battery

CATION An ion drawn towards the cathode

CENTRAL FORCE A force which acts in a straight line between one point (or centre) and another

CHARGE See ELECTRICITY

CLASSICS The study of the Greek and Latin languages and the civilizations of Greece and Rome

CONDUCTIVITY The ability of a substance to conduct electricity

DISCHARGE The removal of an electric charge

ELECTRICITY Electricity is difficult to define, and we only know it is there because of the effects it produces.

Static electricity, or an "electric charge," may appear on an insulator when it is rubbed. An insulator which has been "charged" (such as a dry glass rod rubbed with a dry cloth, or an inflated balloon rubbed on clothing) will attract light objects such as tiny pieces of paper. If the charge is great enough, sparks will be produced.

Current electricity, or an electric current, is electricity moving through a conductor. The presence of an electric current may be detected by:
—the magnetic effect it produces
—the production of heat

—chemical effects if the current passes through an electrolyte

—the production of sparks

ELECTROCHEMISTRY The science of chemical effects produced by an electric current

ELECTRODE A conductor through which an electric current enters or leaves an electrolyte or a gas discharge tube

ELECTROLYSIS Chemical decomposition produced by an electric current

ELECTROLYTE Substance which is decomposed in electrolysis

ELECTROMAGNETIC INDUCTION See INDUCTION

ELECTROMAGNETISM Magnetic effects produced by an electric current in a wire

ELECTROSCOPE A device for detecting the presence of an electric charge

GALVANOMETER An instrument for measuring electric currents

GENERATOR A device for producing an electric current

INDUCTION Producing electric effects in a wire as a result of either a magnet moving nearby (magneto-electric induction) or a varying electric current in another wire (electromagnetic induction)

INSULATOR A substance which does not conduct electricity. Two conductors of electricity are said to be insulated from each other if there is no connection between them

IONS The constituents of an electrolyte which are separated in electrolysis

MAGNETO-ELECTRIC INDUCTION See INDUCTION

MAGNETO-ELECTRICITY An electric current produced by magneto-electric induction

NATURAL SCIENCE This is not "natural history," but what is nowadays usually called "pure science"— physics, chemistry, etc.

OSCILLATING Swinging or moving to and fro, vibrating

SENSIBLE Faraday used the word with its strict meaning of "can be sensed," or "noticeable"

STATIC ELECTRICITY See ELECTRICITY

THERMO-ELECTRICITY An electric current produced in a circuit made of two different metals when the joints are kept at different temperatures

VOLTA ELECTRICITY Current electricity from a Volta's pile or similar device

Further Reading

There have been several biographies of Faraday. The fullest and most recent is:

L. Pearce Williams, *Michael Faraday*, London, 1965.

A brief account of Faraday at the Royal Institution is given in:

Ronald King, *Michael Faraday of The Royal Institution*, London, 1973.

A summary of Faraday's electrical work set in its historical context is given in:

Percy Dunsheath, *A History of Electrical Engineering*, Faber & Faber, London, 1962. (See the chapter entitled: "Faraday's Great Contribution").

Michael Faraday's *Advice to a Lecturer*, mentioned in the text, was published by the Royal Institution in 1960.

Index

Picture Credits

The author and publisher wish to express their gratitude to the following for permission to reproduce illustrations on the following pages:

The Mary Evans Picture Library—22–23, 33, 36–37, 41, 75, 76, 78–79, 80,

The Ronan Picture Library—2, 8, 9, 14, 16–17, 18, 21, 24, 25, 27, 43, 46, 57, 62, 83,

The Royal Institution of Great Britain—10, 12, 28–29, 30, 32, 35, 38–39, 49, 53, 61, 65, 68, 70, 71, 72, 83–84, 86.

The Science Museum—55